The INSIDE-OUTSIDE Book of LIBRARIES

Book of

Paintings by Roxie Munro
Text by Julie Cummins

Dragonfly Books New York

To my parents, who taught me to love books, and to my editor, Donna Brooks, who helped me love to make them—R.M.

To Blair, my favorite librarian—J.C.

ACKNOWLEDGMENTS
The author and illustrator gratefully acknowledge the following people and institutions for their generous help:

Janet E. Baldwin, the Explorers Club; Margueritte Boos, Ocracoke Library; the California Department of Corrections and Folsom State Prison; Sally Campbell, Andrew Heiskell Library for the Blind and Physically Handicapped; Shangyu Chen, Mid-Manhattan Library of the New York Public Library; Mike Dakota, Berkeley Public Library Tool Lending Library; the Denver Public Library Public Relations and Publications Departments; Debbie Gill and Tish Mulkey, Plano Independent School District; Library for the Future; Matt Nojonen, Holmes County Public Library, Millersburg, Ohio; U.S. Navy Public Relations in Norfolk, Virginia; Meredith Mundy Wasinger, Dutton Children's Books; Dr. Terry Webb, Library Director of Kapi'olani Community College.

On page 6, the jacket images of five books translated into Chinese were painted by the illustrator in miniature. Thanks are due to the following publishers for their permission to use these images:

Jacket image from *The Cat's Quizzer* and *The Cat in the Hat* used by permission of Random House, Inc. TM and copyright © 1995 by Dr. Seuss Enterprises, L.P.

Jacket image from *Snow White* used by permission of Farrar, Straus & Giroux, Inc., and Nancy Eckholm Burkert. *Hey, Al* used by permission of Farrar, Straus & Giroux, Inc., Arthur Yorinks, and Richard Egielski.

Jacket image from *Rumpelstiltskin* by Paul O. Zelinsky used by permission of Dutton Children's Books, a division of Penguin Books USA Inc. Copyright © 1986 by Paul O. Zelinsky.

On page 43, the screen image from Kid's Catalog is used by permission of CARL Corporation, a Knight-Ridder Information Company.

Published by Dragonfly Books, an imprint of Random House Children's Books, a division of Random House, Inc., New York

Text copyright © 1996 by Julie Cummins
Illustrations copyright © 1996 by Roxie Munro

Visit us on the Web! www.randomhouse.com/kids
Educators and librarians, for a variety of teaching tools, visit us at www.randomhouse.com/teachers

The Library of Congress has cataloged the hardcover edition of this work as follows:
Cummins, Julie.
The Inside-Outside Book of Libraries/ Julie Cummins ; illustrated by Roxie Munro.
    p. cm.
SUMMARY: Illustrations and brief text present all kinds of libraries, from bookmobiles and home libraries to the New York Public Library and the Library of Congress.
1. Libraries—United States—Pictorial works—Juvenile literature.
[1. Libraries.] I. Cummins, Julie. II. Title. Z731.M947 1996
027.073—dc 20 96-12111 CIP AC

ISBN: 978-0-375-84451-5 (pbk.)

Reprinted by arrangement with Dutton Children's Books
PRINTED IN CHINA
January 2008
10 9 8 7 6 5 4 3 2 1
First Dragonfly Books Edition

CHATHAM SQUARE LIBRARY ❖ Set amidst the busy streets of New York City's Chinatown, this branch library, identified by a blue banner, signifies good things for its community. Chatham Square Library typifies the more than 6,000 neighborhood libraries in the U.S. that reflect their communities' interests and

needs. At Chatham Square, books, maps, newspapers, and recordings are available in both English and Chinese. The library also acts as a cultural center, offering programs and meeting space for community groups and special events.

The children's room in the Chatham Square Library is a lively place—like children's rooms in public libraries everywhere. These preschoolers are enjoying story time with the children's librarian, who is using finger puppets to tell rhymes and tales. Throughout the year, activities featuring crafts, videos,

music, and of course storytelling serve toddlers to teenagers. Whether reading
for school or for pleasure, using the computer, or participating in summer
programs, the neighborhood youth (and their parents) know this library has
resources, activities, and a helpful staff to serve them.

OCRACOKE LIBRARY ❖ The weathered boardwalk here tells of this library's seaside locale: Ocracoke Island, North Carolina, a fourteen-mile stretch of land between Pamlico Sound and the Atlantic Ocean. Although the island has only about 750 residents (who must come and go by plane, ferry, or boat), it is not too small to have its own library. The value of a library is measured not by floor space or number of books but by its usefulness to the community it serves.

The intimacy of the original one-room Ocracoke Library was typical of many throughout the United States—small, friendly places where librarians greet their patrons by name and know their reading tastes. In 1998 the little Ocracoke Library grew into a larger building with an expanded role in the community as a combined school and public library. The library is open from noon to 4 p.m. during the week and from 9 a.m. to 1 p.m. on Saturdays, and is busiest during the summer tourist season. Its collection of about 2,500 books covers a range of fiction and nonfiction for children and adults, with a section of large print as well. Of special interest are books on Blackbeard, a pirate who was killed in 1718 in a battle near Ocracoke in the Pamlico Sound.

THE LIBRARY OF CONGRESS ❖

The splendor of the green-domed roof opposite the Capitol suggests the grandeur beneath it: millions of books and other materials that document our nation's cultural heritage. Created in 1800 to serve Congress, the Library of Congress was originally housed in the Capitol. After the British set that building on fire in 1814, burning all the books, Thomas Jefferson offered to sell his personal library of 6,000 volumes. Congress bought it and erected this impressive Italian Renaissance building bearing his name. As the collection grew, two more buildings were added: the John Adams in 1939 and the James Madison in 1980. The nation's library, the largest in the world, now serves the general public. Its collections continue to grow at the rate of twenty-one new items a minute (or 10,000 per day).

With its ornamental ceiling, stained-glass windows, and statuary, the Rotunda Reading Room forms an awe-inspiring center for the library. A computer catalog and CD-ROM indexes help users find what they are looking for among the 130 million items the library owns. In addition to books, including children's books from 1870 to the present, it has many specialized collections: manuscripts, maps, photographs, movies, and radio transcripts. The library also administers the U.S. Copyright Office, registering books and other original materials to protect the ownership of their creators. Copies of copyrighted books, including this one, are a major part of the 10,000 items added to the collections daily.

Andrew Heiskell Library for the Blind and Physically Handicapped ❖

The cane, the dog, and the wheelchair are the first clues that this library is unusual. Part of a national network designated to serve people with visual and other physical impairments, this branch in New York City is equipped with specially formatted materials and machines that enable users to enjoy favorite books and magazines, study, or just browse. Readers who cannot see regular print have many options here: "talking books" on both disk and cassette, books in braille, large-print books, a Kurzweil machine (which converts printed text into the sound of speech), and closed-circuit television magnifiers that enlarge a page of text up to sixty times.

With his fingertips, this young patron is reading a story in braille, a method of writing that uses patterns of raised dots. Its nineteenth-century French inventor, Louis Braille, was blinded at age three and developed the touch system when he was fifteen. The sixty-three different dot formations represent letters (including capitals), numbers, and punctuation. Using the index fingers of both hands, readers can average about 125 words per minute. The children's room at this library caters to the sense of touch with puzzles, puppets, and tactile objects like jingle bells, globes, and plastic dinosaurs that help visually impaired children identify shapes. Both children and adults can borrow braille and recorded books, as well as audio-playback equipment, for home enjoyment.

The braille here reads: "hard to realize that the rustle of a falcon's wings is . . ." It is from *My Side of the Mountain*, by Jean Craighead George (copyright © 1959 by Jean Craighead George).

Explorers Club Library ❖

This six-story town house in New York City serves as the headquarters of the Explorers Club, an organization founded in 1905 to encourage scientific exploration and to serve as a meeting place for explorers and scientists. Membership is worldwide and includes famous explorers both past and present, such as Sir Edmund Hillary, Admiral Robert E. Peary, and Sally Ride. The club maintains an unparalleled library here—open by appointment to its members and the public—of 25,000 books, maps, and objects dedicated to scientific exploration and fieldwork. Memorabilia, paintings, and sculpture document members' accomplishments and illustrate the conquest of frontiers.

Maps and charts are vital to every kind of exploration, so the Sir Edmund Hillary Map Room on the sixth floor of the town house has collected over 5,000 of them, including early charts and members' hand-drawn sketches of remote regions. All areas and aspects of exploration are covered by the library's collection, which includes books written by members, as well as diaries, photographs, and artifacts from legendary exploits: Admiral Peary's sledge, the globe Thor Heyerdahl used in planning his Kon-Tiki expedition, a giant stuffed polar bear from the Chukchi Sea in the Arctic, and an ancestor totem from New Guinea.

ABRAHAM LINCOLN (CVN 72) LIBRARY, U.S. NAVY ❖ The flurry of activity aboard this nuclear-powered aircraft carrier, one of seven Nimitz-class carriers, seems incompatible with the quiet atmosphere of a library. But the 5,500 men and women who eat, sleep, and work here must also be able to

study and enjoy their leisure time. So in this special world—where every day 18,000 meals are served and 185,000 gallons of fresh water are made—a small but full-fledged library is tucked below the flight deck on the port side.

Books ahoy! In the library aboard the *Abraham Lincoln*, crew members can browse comfortably and check out books, videos, CDs, cassettes, and even computer games. Private work centers offer computers for studying, writing, or other projects. For keeping up with current events, there are newspapers

and magazines. The most popular is *Navy Times,* a weekly publication that reports on military matters, lists promotions and assignments, and carries news and ads as well. The library is next door to the chapel, so the ship's chaplain does double duty as librarian.

FOLSOM STATE PRISON
LIBRARY ❖ Located on the site of
an old gold mine, California's second-
largest prison was opened in 1880 to
relieve overcrowding at San Quentin.
Inside the forty-acre granite-wall
enclosure, a library houses two separate
collections of books for the 3,800 men
to use. Folsom's educational programs
that utilize the library include literacy
workshops, English as a second
language, and vocational training, all of
which give prisoners (three-quarters of
whom are high school dropouts) the
chance to increase their skills and
complete their education. Inmates who
work as clerks in the library earn a day
off their sentence for each day worked.

Without the more than 500 prison libraries in the U.S., those imprisoned would not have ready access to ideas and information. Federal law requires prisons to provide a law library adequate to assist inmates in the preparation and filing of legal papers. Use of Folsom's 5,000-volume law collection has motivated several men to become paralegals after they were released. In Folsom's recreational library, which contains 20,000 books, Westerns are the most popular reading. The library purchases bestsellers monthly and subscribes to newspapers in five languages. It keeps a section of children's books, too, for fathers to read with their children during visiting hours. The library is open daily from 8 a.m. to 8 p.m.

TOOL LENDING LIBRARY
TUES-WED 12-7:30
THURS 1-5:30
FRI-SAT 10-5:30
SUN-MON CLOSED
Please have library card ready

TOOL LENDING LIBRARY ❖ A wheelbarrow, a ladder, and a cement mixer are unexpected items to see lined up outside a library, but at the Berkeley Public Library Tool Lending Library in California, they're as common as books. Begun in 1979, the TLL has over 2,000 home repair and gardening tools available

free of charge to residents age 18 or older who present their library cards. The tools may be borrowed for up to three days. Each tool has its own bar code for checkout, patrons may place reserves, and the library charges overdue fines ranging from $.50 to $15 a day, with additional fees for damage.

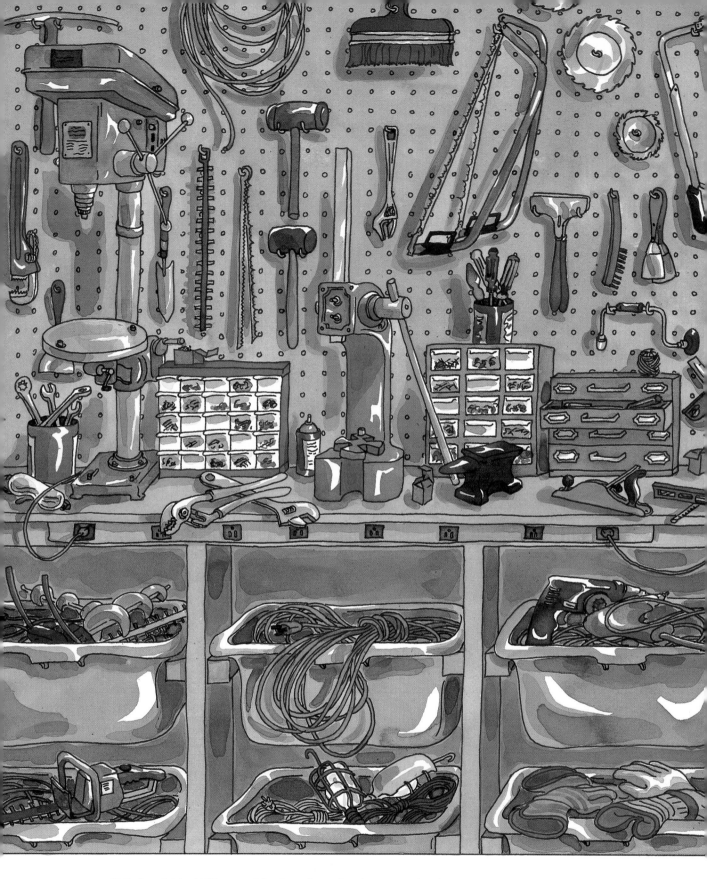

Of the 250 different kinds of tools that can be borrowed, the most popular are Weed Eaters, hedge trimmers, demolition hammers, and electric snakes. From large items like piano dollies and table saws to small tools like drill bits and putty knives, all the equipment is organized and stored according to size and

shape so that the staff can locate each tool easily. The branch library next door adds the finishing touch by offering a sizable collection of how-to books and videos for a wide range of do-it-yourself projects.

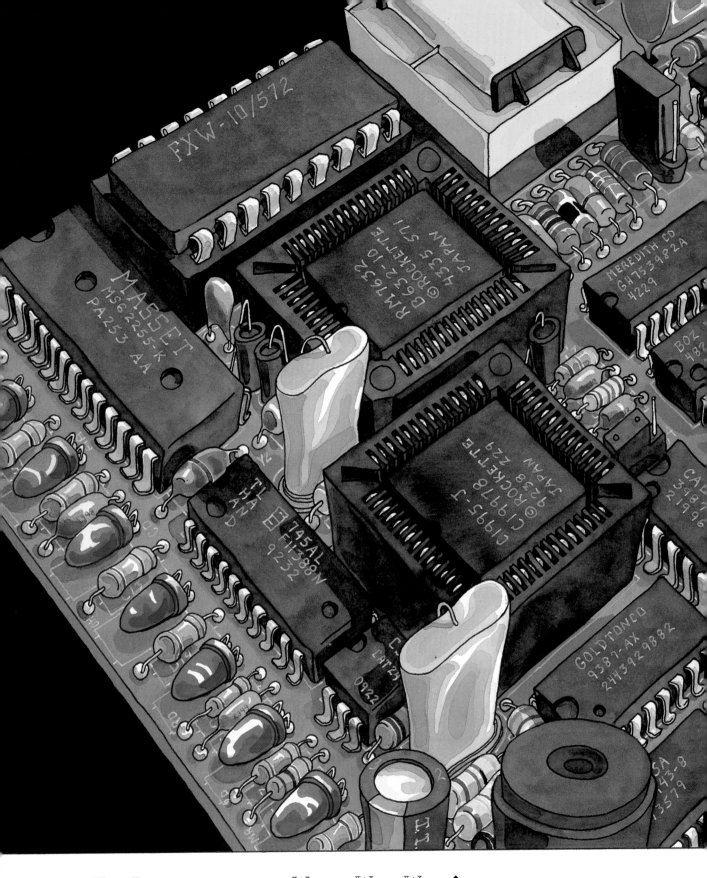

THE INTERNET AND THE WORLD WIDE WEB ❖ This maze of circuitry is the inside of a modem, seen close up. A common use of the modem is to link computer users to the Internet, a network of thousands of interconnected computers around the world at places like universities, libraries, businesses, and government agencies.

A popular way to use the Internet is through the World Wide Web, which allows you to jump from one computer site to another and explore what is there via a series of graphic directories called pages. A mere click lets you read all kinds of text, view pictures, watch animations, or listen to music.

These two students, one at Kapiʻolani Community College in Hawaii, the other at the Denver Public Library, are thousands of miles apart. Yet, via computer, they can tap into the same information. Because the Internet has no geographical boundaries, each can gain access to library catalogs at major universities, read

research papers, look at sports-team home pages, or even contact the space shuttle. Sitting in Hawaii, she could view a photo of an old frontier map from the Denver Library collection; he could learn Hawaiian from an audio file offered by the community college. The Internet constitutes a library without walls.

MEADOWS ELEMENTARY SCHOOOL LIBRARY ❖ "What's happening?" asks the sign in the library of Meadows Elementary School in Plano, Texas. The answer is the bustle of activity these fourth graders create as they look up homework answers, prepare reports, read, and get ready for Children's Book Week.

The 94,000 school library media centers in the U.S. provide all kinds of materials to stimulate students' curiosity and imagination. These children can explore books, videos, science models, computers, and other special items like frontier trunks containing things that convey how Texas settlers lived and worked.

There's a mouse in the school library! But kids use this one to click onto a computer program called the Kid's Catalog. It's a computerized catalog enhanced with pictures and words that help students find books and other materials in their library. Symbols represent categories such as Science, Scary Stuff, and

Famous People. Click, and you see a listing of books the library owns under that category. Or you can click to search for specific titles or authors. Click again, and a floor map appears that pinpoints the exact location of a book.

This school library is up and running!

HOME LIBRARIES ❖ On the outside, these buildings are all different. But inside, they have one thing in common. The families who live here each have a home library. When people care about things they've read or heard—in books or magazines, on tapes or CDs—they want to have them on hand to reread and

refer to. So they keep them, and soon they have a library. Depending on how people use them, books may be found in all kinds of nooks, corners, and shelves around the house—the bedroom, kitchen, family room, hall, garage—even the bathroom!

Your own library needn't be fancy or neatly organized. It can be a simple shelf or even a trunk. What matters is that *you* have chosen the books that are there. Some people keep books in their libraries that they haven't yet read—to look forward to reading. Others look fondly upon their libraries for the favorite

characters and scenes, authors and ideas they've already enjoyed and will enjoy again. Few things offer the lifelong pleasures that books do. From spellbinding stories to true adventure, from humorous poetry to mathematics and biography, books enable us to laugh, to dream, to hope—and to envision the future.

BOOKMOBILES (opening pages) ❖ The first bookmobile was a single horse-drawn van that in 1905 carried collections of books to people living in rural areas of Maryland. As motor power has replaced horsepower, traveling libraries have grown from simple wagons to air-conditioned vehicles equipped with cellular phones, CD-ROMs, and an average of 3,000 books. Today, about 900 bookmobiles make library service available to children and adults in a variety of settings. These mobile units stop at housing projects, shopping malls, schools, and senior citizen homes, as well as outlying, sparsely populated areas. Slanted shelves prevent the books from falling as the bookmobile travels over rough streets or rutted roads.

THE NEW YORK PUBLIC LIBRARY (jacket) ❖ Two marble lions named Patience and Fortitude guard the most recognizable library in the United States—the New York Public Library's famous research building at 42nd Street and Fifth Avenue. Beneath the ornate ceiling of the main reading room, a quarter of an acre in size, 700 people can sit and read. With 88 branches, 4 research centers, and a collection of over 50 million items, the NYPL is the largest library system in the nation, serving over 8 million people annually. The majestic central building symbolizes all public libraries, where everyone—rich or poor, young or old—has equal access to the wealth of knowledge that is our heritage. As a treasure-house of thought from which to project the future, as a repository of ideas both familiar and provocative, libraries safeguard intellectual freedom for us all.